I0482191

Insurance

Best Practical Guide for Risk Management, Property, Liability, Life & Health with Concepts & Coverage.

By James Stevens

Published by Shepal Publishing

Table of Contents

Introduction

There are many different ways that you can lose something valuable to you, and the thought of this loss can leave you distressed, frustrated and confused, wondering how you can possibly recover. To help provide some assurance and security, insurance is an ideal solution. Insurance allows individuals, families and organizations to get protection from financial loss that is caused by unexpected or accidental occurrences.

When you are seeking insurance, you can choose personal insurance or commercial insurance. With personal insurance, you are able to insure your property (which includes real estate as well as personal property) as well as personal liability exposures. In addition, you can insure your automobile, meaning that in case of an accident, you are protected even though you may have caused the accident. The insurance covers the costs of any physical damage that the vehicle incurs, and can also extend to insuring passengers and their medical expenses.

Regarding commercial insurance, the focus is on ensuring that there is financial protection for property that is commercial, industrial or based on business. Various packages are created to protect against crime, breakdown of equipment, injury to workers and any other liabilities.

This book shall clarify how insurance can provide you protection from various risks, and explain how you and your property can be covered from adverse situations. Take this opportunity to learn why insurance is a basic economic necessity, and how it can provide you with immeasurable peace of mind.

Chapter 1:
How Insurance Manages Risk

Even though you may have never had an insurance cover, it is likely that you have heard about insurance. There are many insurance companies that exist in the market, and within the financial industry, these companies are major employers. To ensure that the market is familiar with their products, they send agents out to meet with people and get them to sign up for insurance policies.

The types of policies that are available vary from those that help one to fund their children's education, cater to families in the event of death of a family member and protect assets in the event of damage or theft. Insurance is indeed a way that you can manage your risk for the long run.

The question one should ask is, what is risk? Risk is all about dealing with a threat which could come in the form of an action or an event. Typically, risk could affect an organization in a negative way, and hinder the organization from being able to meets its goals, or fulfill its strategy. When managing risk, it is essential to identify, analyze and also control these possible threats so that the negative impact of risk can be minimized.

Why should risk be managed using insurance? Here is an answer to this question with a practical example.

Consider a shop keeper who has spent his life saving stocking up his shop with goods for sale. He has some basic security, perhaps a metal grill on his door to keep out potential burglars. In addition, the shop is located in a dangerous area or neighborhood which affects the overall safety of the shop keeper's assets. He is constantly at risk of losing his merchandise through theft, or even through violence and looting in the area. To manage this risk, and to ensure that he has peace of mind, he chooses to take out an insurance policy. What this policy stipulates is that in the event that something (within certain criteria) occurs, and there is loss or damage to his stock, he will be compensated and the stock can be replaced.

This example provides a description of insurance in a nutshell. It is all about making sure that one protects themselves and their property from things that could happen to them, negative occurrences. When a person takes out an insurance policy, it is estimated how much a loss would cost, and then a premium (an installment that is paid at stipulated intervals) is paid to cover that possible occurrence. Insurance transfers the risk, so that it is not born by the individual, but rather, by the insurance company.

Risk Management and the end Customer

Insurance is not only designed to manage risk for an organization (in the case of commercial insurance). It also offers the end customer some reassurance that their investments within a company are safe. For example, when you put your money in the bank, you are trusting that the banking institution will keep the money safe. However, there is every possibility that something could go wrong and the bank collapses. In that scenario, you as a customer could lose out and never recover your savings. If you know that the bank you are saving in is insured, then your mind is at ease because you will be compensated should something go wrong with the bank.

Governments also insist that certain companies should have insurance to help manage risk, and for this, they put regulations in place for facilitation of insurance. This is especially true for large companies which could collapse an entire economy in the event that something goes seriously wrong with their operations. In this case, the insurance helps manage risk for the end customer who us assumed to be the government.

Risk Management and Joint Ventures

Companies that are looking to expand by way of a joint venture may choose to take out an insurance policy to ensure that they are covered from risk of things not going according to plan. Typically, when something negative happens, then the company is saved from taking a financial hit that could bring it down.

Looking at these explanations on risk management reveals that insurance for risk is not black or white. Many companies choose to take insurance to manage risks from damage or theft, while others take insurance to positively influence their customers and other stakeholders. When choosing to take a policy for insurance, it is important to converse with your insurance provider to explain the ultimate goal of the insurance policy. This will ensure that you end up with the right insurance product to manage your expected risk. Insurance makes up an important part of any risk management strategy.

The main reasons that companies choose to insurance for risk management is because they rarely have enough reserve funds to shoulder certain risks themselves. Insurance means that when something goes wrong, they have an out, a way that they can stay in operation without making significant operational sacrifices.

As an individual, managing risk reveals that you are aware that the unexpected could happen, and you want to ensure that you are prepared for any eventuality. Insurance is the best way that you can have all your bases covered. Choosing insurance for risk management shows that you are living by the words of the old and wise saying, that prevention is better than cure.

Chapter 2:
Insurance and Property

A large number of insurance policies are taken out to protect individual or commercial property. This is because property often requires an investment, and insurance helps to protect that investment. There are some major investments which people make, such as purchasing a house or a car. Should anything happen to these investments, they may take some time to recover which could be a major blow to the person who purchased them. This is where insurance becomes important.

This is how insurance works. You take out a policy which enables you to pay a relatively minimal fee to a company that provides insurance policies. This payment is the guarantee you need that the insurance company will bear the cost of possible loss of an asset. Insurance for property does not cover every possible loss scenario. Typically, there are specific circumstances that govern that loss, and normally, these have to be uncertain in nature.

Here is an example to clarity this. When you own car, you may pay road taxes to enable you to use the car freely on the road as is stipulated by the law. In fact, as long as you pay that tax you can choose to move around with the car or even leave it parked in one spot. Now, imagine what would happen if one day, a massive boulder fell down on your car. Although you have paid the tax to enable you to use it, without insurance you will face a tough situation. You would have to pay the full repair cost for the car, and this could leave you in a bad state financially. However, if you have insurance, then you will receive compensation for the damage, and can easily replace your car or get it fixed if you wish to do so.

Mandatory Insurance

Most people do not want to take out insurance, viewing it more as an expense than as an avenue to manage risk. Nonetheless, there is some insurance that is mandatory, meaning that one does not have a choice but to take it because this is what the law stipulates. For example, if you own a car, you normally cannot drive it around unless you have taken out insurance. There are various types of automobile insurance, and the one that you choose will cover you for different levels of risk. As you are making a choice on what to get, consider who will be driving the motor vehicle, and how much the vehicle is actually worth.

The same applies for anyone paying for a large asset, such as a mortgage on a home. The insurance helps cover one of the parties from risk, particularly a lender in the event that defaulting a loan is possible.

Insurance Restrictions

Knowing that insurance helps to offer protection from risk may have you enthusiastically looking to insure everything that you possibly can. However, you will find that insurance companies and the policies they give out are very calculated. This is because they are also determined to protect themselves from certain risks. In the event of a major event, without the right protection in place, an insurance company could find themselves out of business.

Therefore, when insuring your property, you will find that the typical policy will normally not include damage or loss from natural disasters such as floods and earthquakes. Negligence, such as that which would cause mold also is not included in many insurance policies. Also left out are acts of war. This is because these events cause damage on a massive scale and providing insurance for this damage is not sustainable for the vent company.

When checking your insurance proposal for property, you will often see that you are insured against problems that are accidental or sudden. What this means is that if you have a pre-existing problem that takes months to manifest to its worst, you may not receive any compensation from your insurance. That is why it is sometimes challenging to make insurance claims on old homes.

So what does your insurance policy typically cover in regards to property? You will normally be covered from fire which damages property, and theft which results in loss.

Property Insurance and Understanding Liability Coverage

When you examine your insurance policy fine print, you will likely come across a term called liability coverage. If you do not see this term, then look for a policy which includes it. This is an important component of any insurance policy, and here is why.

Sometimes, accidents occur which were unintended, and these accidents affect the property of people other than yourself. Imagine that you live in a block of apartments on the second floor. One morning, you leave the apartment to go to work and in your rush to beat the traffic, you leave a tap running. The water runs throughout the day, causing a flood in your apartment. After a while, it starts to seep out and ends up going into your neighbor's apartment. Water reaches an electrical outlet and damages the property that belongs to your neighbor. In this scenario, who is liable for the damage that has been caused?

If you have been paying your insurance premiums, including the liability coverage, then you will find that you are covered and the insurance company will pay for the damage. However, if this coverage was not a part of your insurance agreement, you will be hit with a hefty bill.

Liability coverage extends to more than just protection of property. It also includes protection in case of injury that may happen when someone is on your property. When you do not have this type of insurance, in the event of injury on your property, the injured party may choose to sue you for damages, which may extend to an amount that you cannot afford. For this reason, it tends to be most popular amongst business people in comparison to individuals.

Chapter 3:
Life and Health Insurance

There are two things that you have to inevitably do in your lifetime and those are to go to the bathroom, and to die. Everything else is a choice. When you are using insurance to manage risk in regards to life, you are planning for the unexpected, the possibility that your life may end before you expect it. Most people who take out life insurance policies have families, and they take out this insurance to ensure that in the event something happens to them, their families are well taken care of and able to survive. The first part of this section shall provide insight on everything to do with life insurance.

Why you need life insurance

A life insurance policy pays out something known as a benefit in the event of your death. This is money that is meant to replace the income that you would have been bringing into your home had you been alive. This money ensures that should your family have financial obligations; they can be met. Another reason that people take out life insurance policies is so that their family are able to access funds without fear of deductions due to tax.

When you get married, you and your partner take out life insurance policies, whether or not you have children. The earlier you take out a premium, the lower the fees that you need to pay for this policy. The life insurance policy will help your partner to manage the bills and take care of any accumulated debt in the event of your demise.

As your family grows and children are introduced, a life insurance policy becomes even more important, because the expenses that you incur will inevitable increase. The money that comes from this policy can help a family maintain their standard of living even when the household is reduced to a single income household. This is particularly important if you are a single parent, or if you stay at home to care for your family.

Should you still be on the shelf about whether life insurance is really necessary, ask yourself the following questions,

- In the event of your immediate death, what would happen to the financial stability of your family?

- Could your death leave your family facing considerable debt?

- Would your family be able to afford to live in the home that you have provided for them from your hard work?

- How will the family cater to their daily expenses?

- Is there enough savings set aside to cater for your final funeral expenses?

Thoughtful consideration of the eventuality your loved ones will face makes it clear that life insurance is a viable option.

Life insurance can provide more than just money to help your loved ones in the event of your death. There are policies which mature after a number of years, giving you access to money to live out the rest of your days when you reach retirement age. There are also policies that will pay out a certain amount in funds in phases over a period of years, which can help to supplement your income.

As you decide which would be the best life insurance policy for you, evaluate the different options so that you can make an informed decision. The different types include: -

- Term insurance – This is the easiest type of life insurance to understand and to get. It also has the benefit of being the cheapest option there is. It is called term insurance because the payout is done once you have passed on, and not before. Furthermore, you need to pass within the stipulated term of the policy. For example, you take out a term insurance policy that covers you for 20 years. Your family will not get any benefits if you die after 20 years.

- Whole of Life Cover – Term insurance is restricted with a timeline, but whole of life cover is not. This means that a payout will be made whenever you pass on. This type of insurance is usually linked to another financial asset, most often your pension. Where term insurance was the cheapest option you could find, this is the most expensive cover that you can have. The reason is that no matter what happens, a claim will be made.

- Decreasing debt – This is a life insurance option that has a fixed payout, no matter when it is that you die. With many life policies, the longer the policy has been held, the higher the payout that can be expected. However, with this policy, whether you die within one year or on the twentieth year of a twenty-year policy, your beneficiaries will receive the same amount. You could also arrange for the amount to be paid out to decrease over time, so that the earlier you pass on, the more money your family will receive. This type of insurance policy is usually linked to a mortgage that you are repaying, on the basis that the amount you owe will reduce over a period of time. For this reason, the more time passes, the lower the premium you are expected to pay.

Why you need health insurance

Just like death is inevitable, so is the deterioration of health. The older that you become, the more your health suffers and you may get conditions that are terminal, which often cost a considerable amount to treat. When you consider the fact that you are meant to retire in your old age, you also factor in lost income, and realize that without insurance, you may not be able to cover your health costs. Health insurance gives you the reassurance you need that you will be able to cater to these changes, even as you age. Illness is often unpredictable, so it may be challenging to plan for something that you are not sure will occur, or in what form the illness will take.

On that note, health insurance should not be a priority for those who are aging alone. Everyone should have health insurance as you could get sick at any time, whether you intend to or not. While you are sick, working may be impossible meaning that you may not be able to treat your illness with your normal income. In that instance, health insurance is highly beneficial.

Health insurance is so important that in America, it is mandatory for everyone to have health insurance no matter what their income may be. This helps to prevent premature deaths and suffering from ailments that can easily be treated and cured if there is money available to do so.

So what exactly does health insurance cover?

- It will help to protect you from medical costs that are unexpected. These costs are often high and can overwhelm a person who is not covered.

- This insurance also helps to cover your basic health., so that you are able to maintain it by getting the treatment that you need in case of an accident, or if you contract an illness.

- Health insurance enables you to pay nominal amounts for health care as part of the cost is covered by your health insurance provider.

- When you need preventive care, you are able to access it free of charge, enabling you to go for necessary check-ups without worry.

Since the law requires you to have health insurance, you may face some unpleasant consequences when you do not get this insurance. These include being charges a penalty which you have to pay as tax. The penalty that you pay is much higher than the cost of getting the insurance in the first place, so it makes no sense to take this risk.

In addition, you give up your right to get access to free preventive care. This means that when screening for chronic ailments like cancer or getting essential vaccinations, you do not get the full benefits. This increases the risk of your developing a problem that could cost you your life, and if you do have these illnesses, the cost of medical care could leave you financially unstable.

Health insurance also enables you to offset a myriad of costs, particularly when it comes to your taxes and other expenses. It makes sense to get this insurance, purely because it will help you save more in the long run.

You will get life and health insurance when you are willing to be responsible for your life and wellbeing. This type of insurance shows that you care for what happens to you, and how this can affect the people that you love. It does not matter what age you are, or what stage of life you have reached, and you should not adopt a taboo mind-set when it comes to this insurance. If you want to pay the most affordable premiums, make sure that you take out insurance when you are still you, and cover yourself from risk that is unpredictable and which could cause you harm or loss of income.

Tips in choosing the right life and health insurer

Choosing an insurer can be tricky especially when all of them keep promising good service delivery and the best policies. There is usually no way of knowing who the right insurer is until you get down to business and start researching. If you consider the right factors, you will end up signing up with the right insurer. People need to know that they have to do their homework right if you do not want to make a regrettable mistake when you are picking an insurer. Here are some factors that can guide you and take you to the right insurer:

a) Insurance rates: An insurance company's ratings are a good way to determine if it is a healthy company or not and this is an important thing when you are choosing an insurer. Information pertaining to insurance companies' ratings is easily available online these days. This will also determine the cost of insurance.

b) The size of company: Large insurance companies are mainly those that have been in the market for a long time. Such companies are said to be stable, highly reliable and they have great experience in dealing with clients. Such companies might have a wide range of options in policies to choose from, giving you a chance to make a perfect choice that meets all your needs and abilities. All these indicate that such companies are in a better position to offer better insurance services than the smaller companies.

c) The reputation: This is a good factor to consider if you do not want to experience endless problems with your insurance company in the period of time that you will be dealing with them. There are companies that have received a series of complaints in the past years because of their poor quality services and these are the kinds of companies to avoid by all means.

Chapter 4:
Auto Insurance

Insurance is one of the oddest purchases you will ever make in life. You pay for it and then you live your life wishing that you will never get to use it. No one wants to be in a situation where they will need to use their insurance benefits, that is why a lot of people are satisfied with the fact that their insurance money does not eventually come back. One thing that is inevitable though is the fact that accidents do happen, and they happen to anyone, not just to specific types of people. If this was to happen, you will be happy you had an insurance cover.

Auto insurance is as beneficial as any other type of insurance that is common today. Whether the problem was your own fault or the fault of another person, your insurance company should be able to help you out. The amount of money you will receive as compensation varies though and this is determined by the kinds of options that you have chosen for your insurance policy. It is therefore important to make a good choice of an auto policy so that you will get the kind of compensation that you will be happy with in case something happens.

Auto insurance policies can be very confusing especially to a beginner in insurance matters. Everyone wants total protection but they do not want to pay so much money for the policies. That is why it is important to learn about all the factors that come into play when one is insuring their cars so that you will make the right choice of policy. This will also ensure that one chooses the right type of insurance company to deal with, one which will be there to offer its help and support when an accident happens.

Important factors to consider before buying an auto insurance

1. Personal injury or liability- Before anything else, it is important to take into consideration the most important thing and this is your safety and the safety of your family. That is why personal injury and personal liability are coverages that should be given the first priority in this kind of insurance. If something bad ever happens to you or to your family member, one of the primary factors that will come to your mind is their health and physical wellbeing. If you do not have a medical cover, this will be an important factor to consider in the kind of policy that you will choosing. You will have to go for a policy that will cater for medical expenses, both in a major and also in a minor accident.

2. Major accidents: In as much as you do not want to think about it, you have to imagine the worst case scenario in case of an accident when you are insuring your car. Some accidents can get really ugly. What if your car is totally damaged and you might need to replace it? If it was not your fault, the other driver's insurance cover might pay for it, but imagine another factor that can cause total damage to your car. That is why it is important to think about what can happen, then insure your car with that in mind so as to warrant that there will be no way you will be required to face the problem alone. It is always good to have a coverage that will take care of every damage without being required to pay any other money for it.

3. Car repairs: One does not always have control on what might happen to their car. A car is made from different

kinds of materials and these can easily get faulty. Sometimes you might be stranded in the middle of nowhere with no way to go home just because of a mechanical damage that you have no control of. It is good to be well prepared for such issues so that you will not be stressed out once they happen. Having an insurance cover will be a great help and shall save you from looking for help every time you are stranded. You will end up saving so much money, and time.

4. The uninsured driver: Many drivers who cause accidents on the roads are those that are uninsured. You need to insure yourself against this if you are not ready to lose your car. In as much as you can be careful enough not to cause an accident, you can never say the same for other drivers out there, that is why it is better to be well protected against such risks than come to regret it later on.

5. The quality and the age of your car: The kind of insurance policy you will choose will be determined by this. A new and high quality car for instance will stay stronger for a couple more years as compared to an old and probably poor quality car. For the former types of cars, you can go easy on the towing coverage but you can at least consider the fact that you might face a flat tire issue even on the first year of driving your new car. If some of these benefits are offered by your dealer, you can skip them on your insurance policy, then go for other issues that could cost you money. Always note that a high quality car will be expensive to repair in case of damage. This should also be a major concern when you are buying your auto insurance cover.

6. The premium versus deductible: The insurance deductible amount is used to determine the insurance premium of a certain policy. If the deductible is high, the premium will be down and if the premium shoots up then the deducible will go down. With this in mind, you have to determine if you want to pay more or even less from your own pocket before you can start paying from the insurance. You can choose to pay more as premiums then you will not have to pay more after an accident, or you can choose to pay less as premiums then you will have to pay more after the accident. This is mainly determined by how much money you can afford.

7. The experience of the driver: Insurance companies these days have certain coverage for specific types of drivers. A new driver for instance is prone to making mistakes more than an experienced driver. For such a driver, you can choose a policy that has a good personal liability coverage and a lower deductible. Some insurance companies will charge a higher rate for such a driver. The same goes to experienced drivers who have a track record of past mistakes like accidents and violations of traffic rules.

The kind of auto insurer to go for

Choosing a good coverage is the most important step when one is insuring their car. The next big step is making the right choice of an insurance company to work with. One of the important things that should guide you in this is ensuring that your insurance claims will be paid when the need arises. Some insurance companies will waste so much of your time before they can pay for a claim while others are easy to deal with. You can check out for these qualities in order to end up with the right choice of an insurer:

1. Reliability: you should be able to fully rely on your insurance company whenever you are in need. Most of the reputable insurance companies are highly reliable and will meet the end of their bargain. These are the kinds of insurers you should be opting for.

2. Reasonable: this is in terms of charges. You deserve a good coverage for whatever amount of money that you will be paying for, and your insurer owes you this. Other than this you should not pay more than you should for a coverage that will cost you less in another company. In as much as this does not always happen because of state mandates, some insurance companies will charge a slightly higher price for their services and not improve on the quality of their services. You deserve better.

3. One that offers a full time cover for your vehicle: you cannot be sure about what can happen tomorrow, therefore it is good to be well protected than sorry afterwards. Sometimes it is easier to choose a cheaper policy because you do not want to pay so much money but you will realize how wrong you were once an accident happens. Take your time to research about a cover that will take charge of everything, including out of state accidents so that you will have minimal issues in the event of an accident.

Buying an auto insurance can be a tricky affair. A lot of people do not take time to understand what their policies cover and they regret so much later on. You need to be a smart insurance buyer, one who does his homework well. You have to go into details pertaining to what a certain policy in a particular company covers and what it does not cover. Check out the company's customer service reviews as well to get a glimpse of the kind of relationship you will have if you finally decide to work with them. The company's financial strength should also matter so as to know if it will be in a position to pay for your claims or not when the need arises.

Chapter 5:
Essential Points to Note

Taking out an insurance policy that manages your risks and offers you protection is all about how well you read the fine print. There are certain pitfalls that can be found in policies, and without the proper knowledge of them, you could find yourself at a disadvantage when facing an issue, instead of benefitting from an insurance policy. This is what you need to keep an eye out for.

1. The cover value – Most items have two different values. The first is actual cash value which ensures that you receive the cash amount of whatever asset has been damaged, and the second is the replacement cost. The replacement cost means that anything that has been damaged will be fully replaced. The replacement cost is a much better option than actual cash value. This is because the value of many assets depreciates over time, and therefore, when you get the actual cash value, you may not be able to replace what has been damaged. However, with the full replacement cost, you will be able to get your asset fully repaired or replaced. Although replacement cost premiums are slightly higher, they make excellent sense in time of crisis.

2. Jewelry and art insurance: Normally, when you take out a standard insurance policy for your home, it will cover all the items that are within the home. It is worth noting that when you have high value items such as art and jewelry, you may find that the insurance does not cover their full value. This means that in the event of theft, you do not receive enough compensation to replace them. Therefore, you need to add what is known as a

floater to the standard amount that you pay. This will help cover these items at their full value, and save you from receiving a limited amount, which enables you to replace the lost items.

3. Third party administrators: As choosing an insurance company can be a challenge seeing as there are so many of them in the market, there are a number of companies which are known as third party administrators which help the entire process. These companies take up the position as an intermediary between you and the insurance company, and when you want to make a claim, then you go through them. The problem is that this could affect the amount that you receive in your settlement, as some may be take off to cater for expenses. The process of receiving your claim could also take longer. To reduce all this hassle, it is better to directly interact with the insurance company.

4. Meeting all the requirements: You must take the time to assess the fine print of any insurance policy that you take out, as you often lose out by not looking at the details. Take life insurance for example. You may want to take out an insurance policy in your name and the name of your spouse at the same time. This will require you to have access to the records of your spouse, especially their medical history. Without providing the right information, when it comes time for a beneficiary to make a claim, it may be impossible to access the funds.

5. Factor in expenses: Insurance is far from expense free, and you may find that you are paying premiums or a monthly quarterly or annual basis. You need to look at whether you can afford these expenses for the

stipulated duration of time. With some insurance companies, missing out on a payment could lead to the entire loss of your insurance policy. Also, you need to consider the amount of tax that your insurance policy may incur as this may mean that you receive much less than you expect.

The best way that you can approach insurance is as an investment. What would you do before putting money down for an investment so that you can manage risk? To begin with, you will carefully conduct research on what the investment returns will be, and when you can expect those returns. Your research will also include a critical analysis of the different investment providers so that you can select the one that gives you the most favorable terms. The very same principles apply to the way that you approach insurance.

Make sure to find out what different insurance companies have to offer in regards to their policies, and most importantly, what their terms and conditions are. Ensure that you are able to afford what is on offer. Also, try and get a premium that you can lean on when you are facing financial problems in life, or if there is a major life event that requires financing. Your policy should be flexible, and fit perfectly with what you may need at any given time.

Chapter 6:
Insurance Mistakes to Avoid

Insurance policies are a great savior in case of emergencies. They can help so much in saving your finances. Saving money feels good, that is why anything that will help you save some money however small it can be, should be embraced. However, many people end up paying more than they should for insurance policies. This is because they do not take time to shop around when they are looking for insurance coverage.

Many people think that dropping important coverage or just reducing their coverage is the only way one can save some money but this is not it. It is not even a good way especially if you want to enjoy good benefits afterwards. Do not focus on numbers only but also on the benefits. There is a lot that beginners need to learn in order to ensure that they are saving money the right way as they enjoy the best results in insurance.

Explained here are some insurance mistakes that will cost you a lot of money and prevent you for enjoying good coverage in the end. You should know how to avoid these mistakes too, so as to be happy with your insurance covers:

1. Selecting an insurance company by its rates only: insurance companies will definitely use a low rate to lure clients because they know that this is the way that many people shop for insurance services. There are other important considerations one should make for instance good customer services, its financial standing among others. The insurance rates should be considered but other things come into play in

determining the kind of insurance company that is suitable for you.

2. Insuring a home for its real estate value: The real estate value is not a good determinant of the actual value of a home, therefore insuring your home for its real state value will not be a good idea. In order to get it right, you need to determine the actual value of rebuilding your home and replacing everything in it so that you will get the actual compensation in case something bad ever happened to your home. Do not forget that the real estate value of homes change all the time, therefore this is an unreliable way to evaluate your home. What should matter to you is that you will have your home back and everything else that you own in case of damage.

3. Not asking for discounts: Discounts will help so much in reducing the entire cost of insurance, therefore if there is a way that you can qualify for a discount, it is good to go for it, then let your insurer know that you really qualify for that discount. Discounts that are issued by insurance companies vary from one insurer to the other. You need to know what your insurer terms as qualification for discounts so that you will know how you can go about it so as to enjoy some cost reduction in the end. If it is necessary, you can install an alarm system in your home or car for instance, and then ask for a discount.

4. Selecting a low deductible: When you select a low deducible, it means that you will be paying high amount of premium, which is more than you can recover when you make a claim. Many people do this and they end up making small claims because they do not want to pay

more in extras. Besides, you may be prompted to make small claims which may end up costing you a discount that is claim free, and this comes with a likelihood that your insurer may drop you. You can save yourself by increasing your deductible, which will reduce your premiums and save you a lot of money in the end.

5. Holding on to the same insurer even when changes happen: When you experience a major change in your life for instance you get married, have children, buy a new car or home, it means that you probably need to change your insurance policy. One thing that people do not realize is that the insurer you have been working with for a very long time may not be the best one at that time, and you might need to change an insurer as well. You need to start shopping for the best deals so as to end up with the best insurance cover at all times. The insurance company that offered the best terms so many years ago may not be the best one in the present day, therefore compare rates once more and make the best choice without feeling guilty about it.

6. Ignoring a record of bad complaint: One of the most important things that you should look out for whenever you are shopping for an insurer is its track record of performance. You want to deal with a company with a good reputation but sometimes people are blinded by low rates and other offers to the point of ignoring some of these important details. You need to check out for complaints once in a while just to be sure that you are working with the right insurer. You need to evaluate the weight of the complaints as well and check out if there are other similar complaints about the same insurer before you can think about switching insurers.

7. Dropping an insurance because its price has been hiked. Sometimes this happens. There are insurance policies whose prices are hiked all the time and many people drop them because they do not want to pay more than they were previously paying for them. What people do not take time to think about are the benefits they will be losing if they dropped that insurance and also the cost of a new policy just in case they wanted to drop the expensive insurance for another one. Sometimes it is better and cheaper to go on with the insurance than to drop it. You just have to weigh your options before making a decision.

8. Considering the insurance rules only: The most important thing that people should have in mind at all times whenever they are buying insurance are the end benefits. Many people only consider what the insurer states and his rules of the thumb without considering what they really need. When taking a life insurance for instance, your main consideration should be the income and the expenses of your family in case of your demise. This should be your main guiding factor in the kind of insurance you will go for.

Conclusion

Now that you have reached the conclusion of this book, it is hoped that your understanding of insurance has improved and that any misconceptions you had have been cleared up. Insurance is not an additional cost or expense to add your budget to prepare for something that may not even happen, it is a form of security so that if something does happen, you have everything that you need to cope and recover.

Take note of all the different ways that you can insure yourself and come up with a comprehensive plan. You will find that there are many ways in which you can pay a premium, so you do not have to be overwhelmed with paying for everything at the same time.

In addition, remember to seek premiums which have some flexibility, as this will help you go through tough financial times with ease. Insurance is the best way that you can protect yourself from a range of risks.

Simply think about insurance as an investment that you are making in yourself and your property. Why do you put your money in the bank instead of underneath your bed? The reason is that you trust it will be much safer there and you can still access it when you need it. Why do you insure yourself from all sorts of negative eventualities? Because you know that when the day comes, your insurance can get you out of a sticky situation and help you continue to live your life in the most fulfilling way possible.

www.ingramcontent.com/pod-product-compliance
Lightning Source LLC
Chambersburg PA
CBHW070427190526
45169CB00003B/1452